Learning About Local Laws

UNDERSTANDING CITIZENSHIP

Dalton Blaine

CIVICS FOR THE REAL WORLD™

Rosen Classroom™

rive cars have to
. They can't drive
must always stop

There are laws for people on bikes, too. You need to wear a helmet to keep your head safe.

ınd city has laws.
ɔeople safe
ıe community
ce.

There are some places where you can't ride your bike. It might seem like a silly law, but you still need to follow it.

Some laws make the community better. You're not allowed to litter, or throw trash on the ground.

In some places, there are laws about recycling. Recycling turns old plastics, metals, and papers into new items.

There are laws to keep communities looking nice, too. People have to rake leaves and cut their grass.

When you walk your dog, keep him on a leash. And if he goes to the bathroom, you need to clean it up.

There are also laws about being quiet at night so people can sleep. Laws like this make people happy.

It's fun to learn about local laws. Do you know the laws in your community?

WORDS TO KNOW

helmet

leash

stop sign

trash